Selected Poems

Rob Couteau

Selected Poems

With an Introduction
by Ed Foster

Second, Revised Edition

DOMINANTSTAR

Second, Revised Edition, published in 2025 by
Dominantstar. Copyright © 2021, 2025 by Rob Couteau.
All Rights Reserved.

ISBN 978-1-963363-06-7

The work in this collection is presented chronologically, in order of its composition. The earliest poems date from 1985, the latest from 2020. Over forty selections have appeared in the following publications:

- Blueline
- Footwork
- Mochila Review
- Montague Reporter
- New Leaves Review
- Out of Our
- Passager
- Rockhurst Review
- Talisman
- The Alembic
- The Taylor Trust
- Versitude
- White Pelican Review
- Xanadu
- Z Miscellaneous

Cover: "Woman with a Red Hat" (2019). Oil on Ampersand Gessobord, 14 x 11", by Rob Couteau.

Special thanks to Georgia, Geology Goddess of Patras.

FOR YONGZHEN ZHANG

AND ED FOSTER

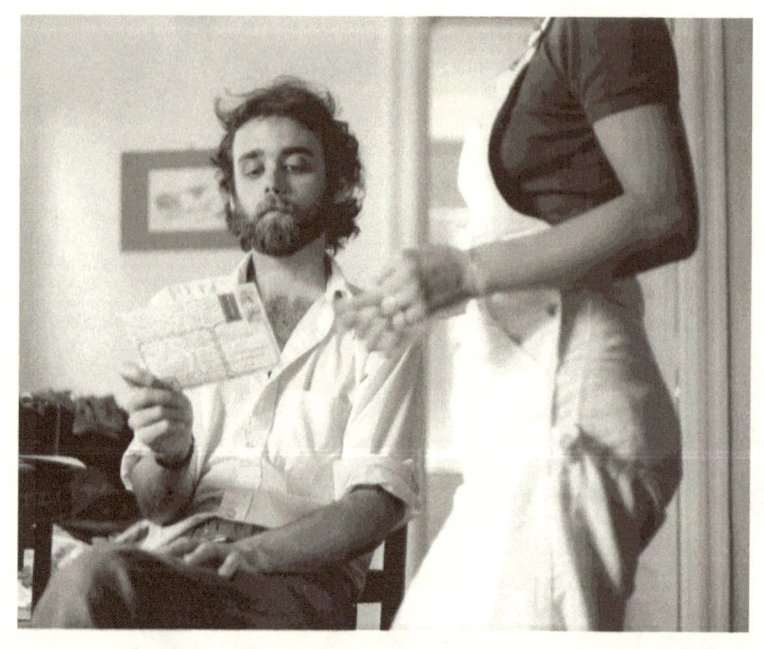

Rob Couteau in Gravesend, Brooklyn circa 1979

CONTENTS

INTRODUCTION TO ROB COUTEAU'S *SELECTED POEMS*
BY ED FOSTER ... vii

BEETHOVENIANA EDDA MARIA ... 1
– Heaven
– Edda Maria soon to leave
– *Beethoveniana* Edda Maria
– Your picture on the wall
– Edda in Argentina
– While you're away
– Angels and imbeciles
– In her white dress
– Bright young gods
– In the shadow of young girls in flower
– Undone
– The existentialists
– Strawberries
– Allen Ginsberg

THE SLEEPING MERMAID ... 25
– To be
– Narcissus
– Blue heron
– Country boys
– Coney Island

– The Sixties
– Advice
– It always shocks me
– The test of time
– Alphabet
– Muser
– The sleeping mermaid
– Apocalypse
– Philosophy in the garden
– Neptune
– The twenty-ninth bather
– Coyote and Beaver
– The girls who wished to marry stars
– Strike
– The one that got away
– Crow girl death
– The cross, a bed of loving nails
– Sylvie
– Cobblestones (*pavé*)
– Rimbaud
– Your ears
– In the white room
– O
– *Femme enfant*, in the grip of dark forces
– Forward, march!
– Portrait of Marie-Thérèse Walter

– Cat and bird chez Picasso
– Jacqueline with crossed hands
– Brassaï
– The weeping woman
– In my world
– Portrait of Dora Marr
– Nothing but
– Homeland
– *Scène de tauromachie*
– A promenade with Walt Whitman
– The black turtle
– Three musicians
– Do you remember?
– O, Queen Venus!
– Night flowers
– Cobra

THE FOOLISH JOY OF THE YOUNG BULL ... 121
– Infinite proposition
– Childhood on Brooklyn streets
– Sainte-Chapelle
– Thomas knew best what he knew least of all
– E. E. Cummings' grasshopper
– Without her
– Haiku for Issa
– Poem for (our) fall
– *Chambre*

– Cosmogony
– Painting haikus
– Haiku for Basho
– The foolish joy of the young bull
– Ibis
– Tree
– From the egg
– The umbrellas of Cherbourg
– The wine of youth

WHAT THE SALAMANDER UNLEASHED … 153
– Wobbling to and fro
– Gardener
– Frozen in time
– Architecture of melancholy
– Hidden portrait
– Princess, snake
– Leaping dogs of the dead
– Why scarab beetles dance on balls of dung
– Portraits commissioned from afar
– Wings
– Where were you leading me?
– A blink of time
– Jaded angels
– Sophia
– Glory sur la quai

Introduction to Rob Couteau's *Selected Poems*

Rob Couteau, in the words of a critic reviewing his novel *Doctor Pluss*, "is not afraid to push the literary boundaries of convention in pursuit of a different form of descriptive truth." Couteau's poetry is marked by a clarity, a crisp directness of vision, and a willingness to violate expected rhythmic and tonal expectations when the poem calls for it. In an early poem, he writes,

> But in the morning
> she's stern and distant:
> she's already three-quarters gone,
> and she stiffens when I hug her
> to say goodbye.
> She knows:
> with such a brutal send off
> I'll think of her constantly,
> wondering if I have her
>   or not,

The "she" is the Argentinian pianist Edda Maria Sangrígoli, with whom, while in his twenties, he was romantically linked. Sangrígoli was and is known especially for her interpretations of the Beethoven piano concerti, but she possesses a distinguished repertoire that includes Ravel, Poulenc, Scriabin, and Rachmaninoff. Poetry should never be read as strictly autobiographical, so much is happening, but it is interesting to imagine Sangrígoli's performances next to Couteau's work. It is as if pianist and orchestra were conversing with each other. Listen to her interpretation of the *Appassionato,* available on the web, while reading Couteau's delicate but impassioned, "Edda Maria soon to leave":

> "Besides, it's good
> you don't kiss me
>   too much.
> Otherwise, I'll miss you a lot."
> And then: "How's your bird?"
> when she means to say *beard.*
> I tell her it's soft
> and would like to rub itself
> along her thigh
> and to be scratched
> by her long
>   fine
>   fingers.

"Edda is good to me; / even in her demands" he continues,

She wants thirty poems
when she returns,
just so she'll know
I gave her thought
at least once a day
all through the month
that she was gone.

Sangrígoli was trained by Vicente Scaramuzza, who educated a distinguished history of Argentinian pianists. Scaramuzza required a total physical relaxation for the pianist in performance. Couteau does not imitate the classically trained Sangrígoli but responds with a complementary relaxed, almost informal sound.

Studying at Julliard when she and Couteau met, Sangrígoli was already established in the European as well as the South American musical worlds. Fourteen years his senior, Sangrígoli "was a fully evolved artist," Couteau has said, "and nearly everything she touched seemed to resonate with music and poetry, whether it involved the way she ground her coffee beans or the manner of her speech. Being able to hear this properly – as a result of whatever I had already learned about poetry – allowed me to transfuse it into a new form of composition that was true to my own experience and expression. And so, by listening to

Edda's voice, I heard my own authentic voice as it welled up in response to hers."

At the time, Couteau was already interested in poets with a high sense of musicality, including Rimbaud, Keats, and Yeats, as well as Eastern poetry and the *Tao te Ching*, with its emphasis on full relaxation in meditative practices. But the crisp directness and clarity in his work may show principally the influence of Sangrígoli.

During the late 1970s and early 1980s, he was also studying the works of Gregory Corso and Allen Ginsberg, particularly their ability to modulate rather than merely imitate what they found in Whitman. Born and reared in Brooklyn, in the 1970s Couteau lived on 11th Street in the East Village, down the block from Ginsberg. Couteau's friend, the acoustic guitarist and song writer Jim Lampos, was Ginsberg's neighbor and, through Lampos, Couteau and Ginsberg became better acquainted. Couteau was drawn especially to Ginsberg's Whitmanesque "A Supermarket in California": "I saw you, Walt Whitman, childless, lonely old grubber, poking among the meats in the refrigerator and eyeing the grocery boys." Remarking later in an exchange with Whitman biographer Justin Kaplan, Couteau argued, "There's not a misplaced word, or beat, or anything"

– in short, an attention to precision much like what he had learned from Sangrígoli.

Lampos and Couteau were both employed in nonprofit agencies established to help the unemployed and homeless, Lampos as a grant writer and Couteau as a case manager and later as director. From time to time they would play hooky from their jobs to help each other improve their work. As a songwriter, Lampos was an ideal professional companion, understanding the need for a gentle fluidity in Couteau's verse.

As a case manager, Couteau was told to avoid talking with his clients about their schizophrenic or paranoid claims. Well versed in Artaud, Couteau found rather that such discussions in fact introduced an understanding of reality that transcended convention and introduced new possibilities, both to his work and to his poetry. Years later in Paris, living on a starvation diet and having difficulty with the rent, he wrote,

> in a white room
> of ten square meters,
> I had what are called
>   visions:
> of golden palaces
> crowning

radiant horizons;
of ancient castles
and lugubrious
fortifications;
of iridescent
reptilian birds
that gave flight
to intoxicating
heavenly mysteries.

In 1985 Couteau won a grant that financed a trip to Paris, to which he returned in 1988, settling there until 2000. In Paris he worked on his novel, *Doctor Pluss* (2006, 2020), drawing on his experience as a case manager while also writing essays and reviews for the *Bloomsbury Review* and other publications. He became friendly with Christopher Sawyer-Lauçanno, then working on a book about American expatriate writers and artists who had lived in Paris and whose poetry bore similarities to Couteau's. Gradually, he made friends and adapted to the culture.

Returning to the United States in 2000, Couteau settled in New Paltz in upstate New York near his alma mater, a branch of the state university. Here he initiated two major projects. In one, the Picasso project, he reimagined works by Picasso, altering brush strokes and coloring. In the second, he interviewed a number of distinguished writers and critics, including Ray Bradbury, Hubert Selby, Justin Kaplan, and his friend from Paris, Christopher Sawyer-Lauçanno. Among those he chose to interview was Sylvette David, who, as Picasso's model, played a role similar to Sangrígoli's in Couteau's poetry. Many of the interviews can be found in his *Collected Couteau* series (2006, 2020), which includes a selection of his essays and reviews.

Other projects at the time included a book about Occupy Wall Street and, more recently, a biographical introduction to the reissue of Stanley J. Marks' classic critique of the Warren Commission, *Murder Most Foul!*, concerning the assassination of John F. Kennedy. He also began work on an autobiography, to which Sawyer-Lauçanno contributed an introduction, noting, "What Couteau is striving to do, and admirably succeeding at doing, is to remind us that our lives do not exist in a vacuum. We are part of our time and time is part of us."

Meanwhile, Couteau continued to work on his poetry, giving it a new emphasis on narrative and the loss of youthful innocence. "The dead may disappear without a trace," he wrote in one piece, "yet some continue to play hide-and-seek. Refusing to vanish, they take refuge in our dreams."

But the relaxed, intimate voice he had learned from
sources as different as the Tao, Lampos, and
Sangrígoli remained. The new work might be quite
dark, a recognition of the loss that time inevitably
entails, yet he also pursued, in his characteristic voice,
moments of high beauty:

> A tree
> > shorn
> of its leaves
>
> offers the sleek beauty
>
> of bark
>
> > in cold
> > > sunlight.

There is a deep tenderness in these words, mingled
with the sadness of age. If one goes back to the early
poems addressed to Sangrígoli, one can find the
tenderness there, too, as it is in his work as a case
manager for the poor and homeless. There is much to
admire in Couteau's oeuvre, but this tenderness
stands out among so many things that make reading
his work clearly an important experience.

– Ed Foster, November 15, 2020

Founder of Talisman House, Publishers, and *Talisman: A Journal of Contemporary Poetry and Poetics*, Ed Foster is one of the most important independent publishers of avant-garde poetry today. A former professor of history and associate dean for administration in the College of Arts and Letters at the Stevens Institute of Technology, Foster was also a Fulbright lecturer at Haceteppe University in Ankara, Turkey, and at the University of Istanbul. The recipient of numerous grants and awards from Columbia University, the National Endowment for the Arts, and the National Endowment for the Humanities, he's also the author of over forty books of poetry, criticism, biography, and literary history.

Beethoveniana Edda Maria

Heaven

When we first met,
Edda was seated at her piano
entertaining the consul
    of Uruguay,
while Natalia,
the famous Montevidian soprano,
was bawling out her Verdi.

Edda's bottom
had shaped her dress
into an enormous
    red pear.
I confessed:
how it had lured me;
how it had inspired me.
She said:
"You should have seen
my ass ten years ago.
It was in excellent form then,
and Mother always said *that*
was the side
I should show."

She said never to slap it,
or caress it quickly
or thoughtlessly:
I should pass my hand
across it slowly,
very slowly.
"That and good coffee
    is heaven."

Edda Maria soon to leave

Edda says she can't come over,
she must arrange her papers
for her trip to Argentina.
"Besides, it's good
you don't kiss me
    too much.
Otherwise, I'll miss you a lot."
And then: "How's your bird?"
when she means to say *beard*.
I tell her it's soft
and would like to rub itself
along her thigh
and to be scratched
by her long
    fine
        fingers.

At this
she giggles and groans,
delighted at the thought,
and for a moment becomes
an unencumbered child,
with the world spinning
    like a plaything
        held casually

in her palm,
to be discarded
when distracted
with no afterthought,
guilt,
or regret.

Edda is good to me;
even in her demands
I can find
a comfortable niche
for my soul.
She wants thirty poems
when she returns,
just so she'll know
I gave her thought
at least once a day
all through the month
that she was gone.

Beethoveniana Edda Maria

Before going to bed
Edda rearranges her room,
and scattered in a pile
I see dozens of clippings:
stories with headlines like
Una pianista argentina
y su triunfo en Europa
and *Beethoveniana Edda Maria*.
They're from Germany, Argentina,
France, England.

"Edda, I didn't know
you were world famous."

"What do you know about me?
You know *nothing*."
Then she adds:
"Not really world famous.
Just famous through
Occidental Europe
and Latin America."

Edda is a modest one.
But in the morning

she's stern and distant:
she's already three-quarters gone,
and she stiffens when I hug her
to say goodbye.
She knows:
with such a brutal send off
I'll think of her constantly,
wondering if I have her
    or not,
wondering how tough she is,
wondering
if she's a bigger loner
than I am.

Your picture on the wall

Beethoveniana,
your picture on the wall
stares relentlessly.
Such a tough,
austere beauty;
your eyes
fill the room
and tell me
I don't know
a thing about you.

While you're away
I'll listen to your favorite,
the Ninth Symphony,
over and over.
I'll have to hear it
at least a hundred times
before the sound
melds to music
and begins to flow.

But you're more difficult
than Beethoven,

and one hundred days with you
would yield nothing.
You dispense your secrets
    like a miser,
your kisses ever cautious,
meting tenderness
in exact proportion
to the short distance
we've traveled.

You're building
this first movement
with a madness and tension
that omits nothing
and that contains all
your great Ludwig
would be proud of.

Edda in Argentina

When I called Edda
   in Argentina
she shouted my name,
surprised to hear from me.
"What are you doing?"
"What else, but writing
poems about you?
How was your trip?"
She was sad on Sunday,
waiting hours alone
   at the airport.
I said the whole city
   was sad:
New York had dropped an octave
as she boarded her plane
for Buenos Aries.

It's true that a city resounds
   with discord
when a soul like Edda
flies so far away,
turning head and home
into something numb

and cold:

Rain tapping
on tin-plated
windowsills,
as Edda walks
beneath lonesome
Southern skies.

While you're away

While you're away
I'll remain all alone:
my squeaky fan whirling
while the boys bounce
    their balls
in echoing midnight
school yards.

When you return,
you'll metamorphose
with moon in Scorpio
    as I slip into you,
eyes silvered
with crescents
under Pluto's deep
    black
        pitch.

Angels and imbeciles

Angels are men
like Van Gogh
who did impossible things
with limited materials.

Imbeciles
are the ones
who made things difficult
for guys like Van Gogh.

In her white dress

Magenta rose-petal
   prints
jiggle and sway,
leaves stirred,
my invisible desire.

Her dress a veil,
hiding her.
I painted every fold,
every crease
a tortured longing:

Unspoken words
   tremble
beneath her train.

Bright young gods

Locusts screech
as seasons turn
against us.

Bones soften;
flesh grays;
everything falls
    to ash.

Life is exhausted
between four yellowed,
crumbling walls.

But the girls laugh
like bright young gods
and ask:

Why worry?

In the shadow of young girls in flower

Lingering in shadowy
    courtyard
of St-Julien-le-Pauvre,
Alison leans upon a rusty
    black gate,
drinking cheap wine
and smoking cigarettes
with her girlfriend.
When she sees me
she comes running,
her red skirt rippling
in soft Parisian breeze.

I turn to Joe and say:
Look carefully.
It's not every day
an eighteen-year-old Tasmanian
    comes flying
through Parisian streets
so happy to see you.
And Joe laughs because
he knows it's true.

Undone

Painful labor
of fleshy embodiment:

To grow old
is to become undone,
as a steed gallops
     toward a task
  none dare
imagine.

The existentialists

Watching home movies
with my father,
something catches his attention:
"I'll never forget that wallpaper,"
he says, "how difficult it was
to take down."

"You notice the most
peculiar things."

"Well, that's all life is:
putting up wallpaper
and taking it down again."

The thing is
he's dead serious,
and because of that
I've never had to read
the existentialists –
Dad's bleak vision
has taken me
far beyond
    mere philosophy.

When it's time to leave,

he stands on the stoop
to watch my figure recede
    into the night.
As I turn a corner
and travel back to Europe,
I think of how he makes
the existentialists look:
Churning out philosophical
manifestos is one thing,
but growing up with Dad
in Gravesend, Brooklyn,
is something else.

Strawberries

Uncle Bruce is dying:
his head hangs,
his hands rest:
one on each knee.
He's quiet,
expressionless,
beyond anything
I know
about the end.

He grips a small square
of paper that reads
Strawberries
and asks my father
if he remembers
the strawberry cake
their mother used to buy
at the bakery.
The strawberries were big
back then,
now they're too small, he says,
placing thumb and finger
together to show me.
Then he stares
at me and laughs

as if it's the funniest thing.
Apropos to nothing,
he adds:
Language was invented
by those who wished
to deceive you.
When I ask,
"Where did you read that,
Uncle Bruce?"
he raises an eyebrow
and says, "I don't know,"
and laughs all over again.

Allen Ginsberg

Allen Ginsberg
I miss you:
psychedelic,
clown faced,
bardic old man
    boy
crawling
like cockroach
in & out
of Lower East Side
bodegas
that are immortalized
in your verse
and flourish
like a permanently
rent-controlled
Mannahatta
that exists only on paper,
with Peter Orlovsky
raving about your cock-
roach
ghost.

The cops call Peter
Captain
as they haul him away,
as if locking up
every last trace
of your wondrous
bedbug splendor.

The Sleeping Mermaid

To be

To be young
and possess
the form
of a god,
the mind
of a golem,
the stamina
of a jackrabbit,
the clarity
of mud.

To be old
and lust
for the footfall
of deity,
the simplicity
of illusion,
the rabbit
and its glowing fur,
the reassuring
embrace
of earth.

Narcissus

She was jealous
of the seasons,
of the mountains
that scraped
heaven's door,
of the spectacle
of ocean waves
that crashed
    and foamed.
She brooded
over clouds
that could so easily
shift their form,
and when the sky
cleared she howled,
dismayed to find
a blue
deeper and truer
than her own
icy orbs,
now a ruby red,
enraged.

Blue heron

A blue heron
stares sphinxlike,
then glides away,
barely flapping
    its wings.
It sails just inches
above the water
till it reaches
the opposite shore.

It's a sunny day
on campus.
Now and then
a gaggle of girls pass
and cackle louder
than the geese.
I could speak with them
for a billion years,
yet five minutes
beside the heron
eye to eye
in preternatural silence
would deliver me
far closer
to the truth.

The heron knows better
than to let anyone near.
It takes off well before
   my approach,
while the girls and geese
seem unfazed,
allowing me to pass
without appearing startled.
But the instincts of the heron
are made of finer stuff:
he knows I carry death;
he smells it
from the far shore
as he gobbles a fish
and lives
in wary celebration
of yet
   another day.

Country boys

Country boys
fingerpick guitars
while ducks splash
or float indifferently.
In Gravesend
there were gutters
    and puddles,
no lakes or rivers.
Killer dogs,
diseased rats,
scrawny sparrows –
no deer
or swans
or egrets.
Instead of lush woodland,
a few scraggly trees
reaching heavenward,
their roots swelling under
concrete and asphalt:
like us,
struggling to survive.

Years later
when I returned,
all the trees were gone,

buried in memory,
legendary rustling specters,
while country boys
fingerpick
and ducks splash
under verdant foliage.
Minus asphalt
or concrete ballast,
minus terror
or despair,
their voices
ring hollow
and easy.

Coney Island

As a boy
in Coney Island
I built castles
in defiance
of the long arms
of the ocean,
perplexed
there was nothing
I could do
to forestall
its wrath.

Destruction
to all moats
and fortifications;
destruction
to all towers
and crenellations;
destruction
to all parents
and children.

The arms of the ocean
reach even now
encircle me

encircle you
there is nothing to do
but build castles.

The Sixties

In the Sixties
I attended St. Mary's
Elementary School
and was taught
by anorexic nuns
dressed in medieval
black and white,
as sexless and soulless
as Jell-O.
But then,
in the 6th grade,
two new nuns appeared:
Sister Maryjane
and Sister Magellan.
They were younger
and feistier than the others,
and a playful restlessness
    animated
their lucid regard.

After lunch one day
Magellan entered
the classroom
carrying the skeleton
    of a fish.

She held the bones
as if they were made
of finest porcelain
and said, *Look!*
And astonished we saw
the handiwork of cosmos:

Like Blake's fiery
dynamos of light,
bones exquisitely
shaped and contoured,
shouting with a touch
    of genius.

That day they taught me
something no priest
or soothsayer
could ever teach,
and they did so
with flames of compassion
burning
in their unfettered eyes.

Advice

Pee standing up;
compose sitting down;
make love
every which way;
seek advice freely,
but follow only the knife
as it pierces
the heart.
Surrender yourself
to anything that amuses,
but surmount only
those obstacles
that lend you dignity,
even in defeat.
Never pursue
superficial beauty
in lieu of a homely flower
that will blossom
just this once.
Always judge a man
by the woman
he dreams of defiling;
ignore those
who will never hear
the sound

of one hand clapping;
honor those
who regard you
highly,
no matter how
you may stumble
and fall.

It always shocks me

It always shocks me
when someone acts
reasonably.
Insanity
is rife
in the cosmos:

A yellow jacket
tries to sting
when it could just as easily
    fly away.
Mothers crucify children
    with screams;
fathers burn in pyres
    of frustration.
Our flesh crawls
or else creeps,
but every now
and then
a tender voice
or gentle smile:

No ulterior motive,
no trapdoor,
no guillotine.

And this
leaves me
speechless.

Alphabet

The shadows
of the evergreens
    flow
like an enormous script:
ancient alphabet
scrawled across
lush October grass.
It speaks to me,
yet I cannot
decipher it.
Under fading light
of stubborn
Indian summer,
the darkening shapes
portray worlds
gained and lost,
yet everlasting
in their wonder.

Suddenly a young girl's
    laughter
peals across the lake,
her lips aglow
under sun-dappled
branches.

As she laughs again
I wonder if spears
   of grass
are tickling her feet,
or if she's amused
by some secret
revelation:
a message
only she
can fathom.

Muser

One day she requires
a quiet place
in the corner:
comrade
of a fat spider
and its silver lace.
Another,
the flamboyance
of the sun,
with its overbearing
    gilded face.
The moonlight always
falls too late;
by then, she's vanished
to the other side
    of the gloam.
But something always
urges me to seek her:
under a creaking bough
of a weary evergreen
or in its twisted,
brittle cone.
I follow her scent
in the morning arbor
or in the ancient perfume

of a croaking,
festive lagoon.
Yet all the while
she treads beside me,
and I'm forced
to tease out
every silently
inspired line:

... *Muse* ...

She is constant,
like a steady stream;
only my cup
may falter.

The sleeping mermaid

A sleeping mermaid
washed ashore:
dirty-blonde locks
streaming to her waist,
seven feet tall
from head to fin,
breasts pale as moonlight,
full and round
and undulating
with the natural
ebb and flow
of the tide.
But when she breathed
the filthy air,
her tail transformed
into two long legs
balanced
on a pair
of black stilettos.
In her blue jeans
and tight emerald T-shirt
adorned with sequined
starfish,
she bedazzled
the brine-encrusted fishermen

who tried to drown her
with endless shots of whiskey,
poking and prodding
and hoping to force her
to entertain
like a trained seal
in a mud-brown
back room.

When she awoke,
nearly choking
in a warm pool of blood,
the men were pinned
to the floor planks
by an enormous trident,
diamond tipped
and wreathed
in seaweed;
and the mermaid,
now fully awake,
proceeded
to the ocean.

Apocalypse

One night after work,
Slim and I wander
through a grimy labyrinth
of desperate streets.
On a desolate corner,
glittering with shards
    of glass,
we encounter a young girl:
thirteen, fourteen,
fifteen years old?
She's thin, limber,
a string bean.
She wears tight white shorts
    and a red tube top.
Her hair is carefully braided.
Her skin smooth,
a shiny dark chocolate.

When she sees us
she smiles,
offering to have sex
for just a few dollars.
She's hoping to buy
some crack.
We try to talk sense

into her, to convince her
she doesn't have to do this.
She's amazed: so grateful
to receive our attention.
Perhaps for the first time,
someone's addressing her
without wanting
something in return.

She radiates innocence.
Her smile is shaped
with naive wonder.
Of course, nothing we say
will change a thing;
she's hooked for life.
She'll probably die soon,
a matter of weeks or months,
while we chat so amiably,
as if planning
a high school prom.

All around:
shattered bricks
scattered in heaps,
but no industrious Germans
to sort them.
Apocalypse,

to the horizon.

And now,
I'm certain
that she's ashes.

Philosophy in the garden

Wandering through
the Brooklyn Botanic Garden
on a rare outing with my father.
Surrounded by tropical flowers,
we silently breathe fragrant
   greenhouse air.
I study an exotic
floral masterwork:
exquisitely painted
and perfumed,
a product of eons
of creative genius,
replete with color
harmonies
that only an artist
can perceive
and thus be led to wonder:
by whose hand
did this flower poem
come to be?
But my father
brusquely announces:
"The world will end
in fifty years,
if not sooner.

I don't give it much longer
   than that.
Biological warfare,
nuclear weapons:
sooner or later,
it's bound to occur.
Man's evil …
there's no accounting for it.
It's deep, vicious, worse
than any animal."

Reflected upon the greenhouse
glass I perceive the genesis
of my entire worldview.
On the one hand,
my mother's mystic
Celtic vision:
rapturous,
life affirming.
On the other,
my father's existential
   venom:
a torturous vision
of the maelstrom.
Betwixt the two,
I generate
a philosophy.

Neptune

Neptune
is exacting
a heavy toll.
He conjures sirens
but then discards them
with the jetsam
and flotsam
    of seaweed
and squalid
spume,
while a seahorse
laughs and strokes
a curving reed
with its glistening tail,
and the ocean rounds
    a pebble
with its everlasting
    lament.

The twenty-ninth bather

"Dancing and laughing along the beach
came the twenty-ninth bather,
The rest did not see her,
but she saw them and loved them."
(Walt Whitman, *Leaves of Grass*.)

Whitman was the twenty-ninth bather
disguised as a frowsy maiden.
Through her eyes he relived
every sunbeam,
every glittering stream
   of water
beading down
the young men's
      breasts.

And he lifted his Victorian skirt,
and waded knee-deep,
and touched the bathers unseen,

radiant

in his delight.

Coyote and Beaver

Coyote was in the mood
for rabbit stew,
so he cooked up
a mischievous scheme.
Visiting his neighbor
old gray Beaver,
he said: "I am bored
and in search
of adventure.
Let us go hunting,
each accompanied
by the other's wife.
Whoever kills
the most rabbits
will sleep
with the other's mate.
Then we shall all
feast upon rabbit."

Old man Beaver,
ever wary of Coyote
and his tricks,
scratched his tail
and pondered.
But knowing

he was by far
the better hunter,
he agreed.

The next morning
Beaver rose with the dawn
and, accompanied by Coyote's
comely young companion,
he chased rabbits
while Coyote snored:
sleeping till the sun
circled directly
overhead.

Upon waking,
Coyote visited the lodge
of Beaver's gray-haired wife.
But instead of killing rabbits,
he playfully chased her
round the bed;
and sliding into her,
he made her cry
till she howled
like a Coyote
in contentment.

As the sun kindled

the horizon,
Beaver arrived
with a sack
full of rabbits.
Coyote pretended
to be crestfallen.
Shrugging his shoulders,
he displayed an empty sack.
Beaver grinned and said:
"Now, I will take your wife,
then we shall feast
upon rabbit."

This was how
Coyote enjoyed
rabbit and beaver
all
without lifting
a paw.

Inspired by the Cochiti version of "Coyote and Beaver
exchange wives."

The girls who wished to marry stars

In the Ojibwa village
there were two girls
who were known
as the strange ones.
Instead of sleeping
in the sheltering wigwams,
they slept on the open plain,
far away from the tribe,
under a glittering
blanket of stars.
One night they asked
    each other:
Which star
would you like
    to sleep with?
The handsome red one,
or the clever white one?
"Oh, the red burns so bright;
I'm sure he's the strongest
warrior in the sky!"
"And the white burns
    so pure;
I'm certain he's the wisest!"

They continued stargazing

till they fell
into a profound slumber.
When they awoke,
they were startled
to discover they had entered
a faraway world
where red and white stars
assumed the form of men
and beckoned the girls
to draw near.

The warriors were large
    and powerful,
wiser and more handsome
than they could ever
have imagined,
and they burned so brightly
that the girls
were nearly blinded.

"Come closer," they said,
"and caress my warrior
    manhood."
The girls grew frightened
but were unable to resist,
so they touched
and held the creatures

until the warriors transformed
into shooting stars ~
curving across the milky heavens
and disappearing from view,
leaving the girls to ponder
their lonesome fate
in this vast celestial vault.

After some time
they came upon
a regal woman seated
upon an enormous throne.
When she rose to greet them,
they could see
    a hole
beneath her seat
that looked directly
into their Ojibwa village.
There they saw men
preparing to hunt,
women cooking meat,
and children at play.
And this world,
which had once seemed so stale,
now seemed more wonderful
than the mysterious
realm of stars.

So they began to weep.
But when their tears
touched the toes
of this wizened matriarch,
she was moved to cry out:
"Never before have I felt
such raindrops of sorrow
falling from ruddy cheeks
of lost Ojibwa girls!
You have watered me
like a shriveled plant
and, once again,
I feel a warm glow of life.
So, I will grant your wish
    to return."

Suddenly Coyote
leapt from the Earth
and sailed through the hole
    in the sky,
landing at the feet
of the weeping girls.
"Hold tight
to my testicles,"
he instructed them.
"Red-star girl
    on my left;

white-star girl
   on my right.
When I leap again,
your feet will touch
the sacred earth,
and you'll return to human form."
So they encircled their arms
round Coyote's haunches,
and, gripping his hairy sack,
plunged across
a starry firmament,
finally descending upon
soft and sacred earth.

Now all was well
except for a terrible burning
in the palms of their hands.
"You have touched the stars
and, thus, are eternally
wounded," said Coyote.
"But each night,
if you fondle my member,
your pain will be assuaged,
and life will grow
increasingly bountiful."

So the girls returned

to their tribe
and no longer dreamed
of unobtainable stars
but instead stroked Coyote
and found their pleasure
upon the warm
rich earth.

Inspired by the Ojibwa version of "The girls who wished to marry stars."

Strike

Timmy's father
was known as Big Jack,
and he was the meanest
motherfucker on the block.
A switchblade was tattooed
    to his forearm,
and he wore a black scowl
on his unhappy
cigarette-puffing face.
He was a trucker
who disappeared
for weeks at a time,
but when he returned
you knew it;
because then Timmy
would get his ass whipped
for the slightest of infractions.

Timmy's sisters
were also strapped
by Jack's leather belt.
But since Timmy
was the only boy,
he bore the biggest
welts of all.

For, no matter how hard
    he tried,
he never measured
up to the pathological
standards of his twisted
and demented father.

We were playing stickball
one day when Timmy
struck out.
Jack's voice boomed
across the pavement:
"Timmy!
You're embarrassing me!
Get in the house!"
He was punishing his son
for missing the ball,
forcing him to sit out
the game on this magical
Saturday in the summer.

I was up next,
but instead of walking
to the plate
I called the teams
into a huddle.
To honor Timmy,

I decided that we'd all
go on strike.
United in our hatred
of his father,
we were resolved
to stand up to the beast.
We leaned against
parked cars,
rechalked the bases,
made small talk.
Sometimes we chanted:
"We want Timmy!
   We want Timmy!"
But mostly, we just waited.
As the minutes ticked by,
we felt bigger,
stronger,
better
than Big Jack.
We could see his bulging eyes
burning
behind the venetian blinds:
   staring
but not comprehending
our respect for his son
and our contempt
for the tattooed beast.

After an hour,
Timmy was released
and the game continued.
I don't recall
who won or lost.
It didn't matter
because, united,
we'd defeated the old man
and, once vanquished,
he was unable to reclaim
      his power.

When Timmy married
      and had kids
he never laid a hand on them.
The last time he spoke
to his dying father,
he said he'd never
raise them the way
that he'd been raised.
By the end of the day,
Timmy was the winner,
and Big Jack was no longer
in the game.

The one that got away

There was once a girl
who developed a fondness
for a handsome dog,
and what wasn't there
    to admire?
Strong of snout
and painted
with deep-umber eyes
that watered with love,
the beast followed
this fair maiden
round the Malecite village
till she brought it home
and showered it
with such affection
that it transformed into a man
and became her devoted
    husband.
"Never tell the others
that I once roamed wild
as a four-legged creature,"
he begged his wife.
"Never speak of it."
So together
they kept his secret,

until one day
when they encountered
a pack of wild dogs
    leaping
in heated pursuit
of a ravishing young bitch.
When she asked her lover
if he'd care to join them
he said yes,
so she allowed him
to transform again
    into a canine.
With tongue slobbering
he chased the bitch,
barking happily
through the streets,
never to return.

Inspired by the Malecite version of "The girl who
married a dog."

Crow girl death

Oh,
what I could do
to your long
lady legs!
How your hair shines
pure black
and frames
those tender
petals!
They absorb
my potion
as I turn you
over
and fill you
up.
You cry
like a crow,
flying high
and feeding
upon my carrion,
pecking me
with soft kisses
to death.

The cross, a bed of loving nails

As Rimbaud says:
Nailed to the cross
   by all those
      who loved me!

Exclamations of love,
like spears slicing
my heart!
Fingers of love
squeezing heart,
gripping heart,
till it nearly
stops beating!
Toes of love
curling in the heavens
above a bed
of love:
a million
upturned
nails!

Houdini of love,
I escape
it!

Sylvie

Sylvie,
you're dead and gone;
how can I reconcile
this with the image
of you hovering
one late afternoon
by your lilac door?
It creaked open
as you stood there naked,
your emerald eyes
and platinum blondeness
    irradiating
the musty French corridor;
your skin so luminous,
never foiled
by a corrupting sunlight.
You were just a simple girl,
you said,
a fisherman's daughter.
You didn't belong there
on Devil's Island:
Paris of everlasting cruelty
    disguised
as sophisticated charm.
A country girl who hated

the rank smell of fish.
That drove you to Paris,
where each day
I lowered my nets
and came up with nothing
but the infuriating glow
of treacherous mermaids
and sirens
with calculating,
　　ruinous dreams.

Phosphorescent Sylvie,
your eyes darted
so nervously:
unsure you'd ever
gaze upon a mirror
that faithfully reflected
the purity you carried
like a terrible burden.
You understood nothing
　　else but that:
guided by simple kindness
through a mist-bedeviled
village ever rotting
with despair.
You're dead now,
but you hover beside

that enameled portal
on rue des Boulets,
always greeting me
with an unpretentious
beatitude of flesh,
the only Parisian
sans persona.
Once you were crazed,
confused,
    half mad:
the French made certain of that.
Yet only in your troubled gaze
did Paris make any sense
    to me:
the girl who shamed
mermaids and sirens,
and who shocked
    death
with the open-handed
generosity
    of her greeting.

Cobblestones (pavé)

When wet,
the *pavé* echoes
with a human sound
as Isabella moans,
delighted flesh
upon flesh,
and burps
her homemade
Portuguese wine.
Sound of John Lee Hooker's
Mississippi Delta blues,
    incongruous
in austere Paris gloam.
Sound of a wine glass
    – *clink* –
and Isabella's heels
skimming the *pavé*
as she runs to catch
the last métro.

Sound of a coin
    bouncing
off windowpane
when she returns
the next day,

her laughter animating
the glistening stones
that bear us
patiently
away.

Rimbaud

Rimbaud such a brat,
with his colorful
    syllables
and alchemy of deceit,
his pale butt
rising
full moonish
for Verlaine's
aged
    puttering
        rocket.
Rimbaud
the ancient mariner,
steering a drunken boat
without compass,
pilot,
or navigator,
following
a primal pulse
of creation:

the dawn's
original
    light.

Your ears

Your ears,
floppy and oversized,
are the most human part
of an otherwise perfect
    anatomy.
The boys hoot and howl,
slobbering through
rancid streets,
begging you to pet them.
Alabaster flesh
with goblets of joy
on your heaving chest,
your puckered lips
and pulpy fruit
intoxicating;
but your ears,
like exaggerated
Picasso curves,
    draw me:
I know they absorb
an otherworldly octave;
I know
they can hear
me.

In the white room

For two years
I barely survived
on cheap potatoes,
shriveled carrots,
or a slice
of stinking Camembert.
But this was where
I wanted to be:

In Paris
in a white room
of ten square meters,
I had what are called
    visions:
of golden palaces
crowning
radiant horizons;
of ancient castles
and lugubrious
fortifications;
of iridescent
reptilian birds
that gave flight
to intoxicating
heavenly mysteries.

The concierge knew
nothing of this,
nor did I offer
an explanation
for my seemingly
strange behavior.
Instead,
I tucked a 100-franc note
into a card
and slipped it
under her door.
At least I had the key
to that mystery solved.
Unlike other expatriates
who waited months
for mail
that never arrived,
mine was delivered
promptly.
But the letters I received
from the homeland
were mere gibberish.
I understood only
the glimmer
of ancient silver
and gold,

and birds streaked
with blood-red rainbows
whose talons
never gripped

the earth.

O

I sat her
on the table's edge
and promised
just to look,
not to touch;
for her entire future
as a chaste
Algerian bride
depended on
my good
intentions.
O
she spread
open
O
what a sight!
O
Lord,
you are
a sly
and mischievous
genius!
I'd never seen one before:
her hymen!
As finely woven

as a goddess's veil!
As serendipitous
as the divinity's grace!
As elastic
as a soap bubble
about to pop!
O
hymen!
We should all
sing daily
your
praise!
Finest silk!
Earthworm's
jealous lament!
Thrust of manhood
and you've vanished!
O
fanciful
red balloon
billowing
in amusement park
of my eternal
delight
!
O
!

Femme enfant, in the grip of dark forces

Your seed was corrupt
even before it was formed.
You rose from ashes
   of dung,
yet even the beetles
   avoid you.
You bring only
exclamations of shock,
horror,
and dismay.
When your mother
patted your head,
a hole broke through,
and you fell into a magma
at the center of the earth.
Like a flower watered
too often with tears,
your roots are rotted
and worm-filled,
and they exude
an unctuous poison.
Your lips are swollen
   and comely;
and your eyes
are stupendous orbs

of blue diamond,
but venom laces
your tongue
and ice clings
to your hollow gaze.

I spit upon
your treacherous face,
and my spittle adheres
and boils you
alive.

Simple goodness
is too much
for you to overcome.

Forward, march!

Encased in a suit
of brittle white bones,
I follow the boom and roar
of the freshly minted dead.
A vast and innumerable
    army,
we hold flowers of steel
and march in umber
shadows of sunlight.
Children, cripples,
and tortured old men
swell our ranks;
yet our song
is an unrelenting
joyful cantata.
Here, one truly feels
alive again
as we cast off
our skeletal remains,
play dice with them,
toss them like boomerangs
    at falcons
that spit colored poison,
or pulverize them
into intoxicating parades

of dust.

Marching toward the crater
of a full beaver moon,
we are molded
    into puppets,
or set like sapphire
on a somber gold lattice,
or planted once more
like idiotic seedlings
in a ripe
and fertile garden.

Portrait of Marie-Thérèse Walter

Although she knows
he carries a sun
in his belly,
when she poses
for the painter
she is never prepared
to bear its rays.
As she drifts to sleep,
Marie-Thérèse
remains unaware
that her thighs
have metamorphosed
into viridian fields
laced with frosted
white glaciers,
or that her breasts
are tropical melons
of cadmium red
    and green.

Only her lemon-yellow hair
retains an earthly hue.
As she caresses
an olive-colored leaf
she twists like a whirlpool,

shimmering in moonlight.
Then the sun bursts
through a French window,
stealing the color
of her curls
and framing
her erotic glow
with countless spears
of shameless light.

Cat and bird chez Picasso

A cat stands stiff,
rigid as a statue,
its tail pointing
to the heavens
or to some dark hell.
It clenches the earth
    with claws
that resemble fangs.
From its mouth dangles
a wounded bird
    still crying,
its feathered belly
torn apart, a red gash
cutting through
endless dimensions
    of horror.
We know
it is screaming
because its beak
is stretched open,
but we can only
see it,
not hear it.
For a moment,
the cat is all teeth.

Its hold on the victim
is relentless.
Most horrifying of all,
its eyes:

Focused upon this
fluttering prey,
they can see no farther.
Transfixed,
it is determined
to kill
and then eat
the struggling,
hapless
creature.

Jacqueline with crossed hands

Do not be fooled
by her housewife's apron;
its pockets are deep
and stuffed with gold.
Jacqueline was thirty-four;
Picasso, almost eighty.
When they wed,
she approached an altar
constructed
of his Midas wealth.

In her most striking portrait
she sits with fingers interlaced,
held tightly
round her knees.
Her lips are fine,
feminine,
alluring;
but her jaw is strong,
and her eyes brim
with cold, practical
determination.
Her toes clutch the floor
in a wriggling mass
of frenzied curves,

but everything else
is sharp and pointed,
like an obelisk abandoned
to the solitude
of a windswept
Parisian boulevard.

When Picasso died
Jacqueline wandered
through the chateau
at Vauvenargues,
besieged night and day
by a din of clamorous
    hallucinations,
and by his appearance
even in her dreams.

He was begging her
    to join him,
which eventually she did,
her suicide
being the final proof
that while Jacqueline
may have married
for money,
love finally
conquered all.

Brassaï

Brassaï has plundered
the gargoyles
of Notre-Dame …
Blasphemer!
He's even ordered a pigeon
to squat upon
a gargoyle's head
and to stare:
mesmerized
by the looming lens
of that bold
black camera.

With his raven eyes
and flares of satanic
magnesium, Brassaï
exposes the underbelly
of a twisted,
whore-enraptured world.
He renders
a forgotten realm:
of gangsters with dirty
fingernails and molls
who illuminate gas lamps
with the waning spectrum

of dying stars,
their haunted faces
plastered upon walls
etched with graffiti,
and scratched
by ghosts of scowling
adolescent boys.

The weeping woman

When she cries
her tongue is transformed
into a slimy green lizard
that leaps
upon my arm
    and slithers across
        my naked flesh.
Dora's eyes spin
like colored tops,
and her tears resemble
darning needles
weaving a tapestry
of liquid horror.
She grips a purple
handkerchief
as if it's a hand grenade
and her eyes explode
into a shower
of silver spears.
Her arms flail
as her gaze turns
    upward,
demanding some heavenly
redemption,
but her heart sinks

like a stone anchor
into a leaden sea.

In this delirious commotion,
    she is reborn.

The leaves of the weeping
woman's tattered soul
    unfurl,
like lush green banners,
and her face blossoms:
sure and steady
with the new drama
of dawn.

In my world

In my world
there's so much happening
   all at once:
Blakian tygers
burning through the night;
paying the electric bill;
butterfly metamorphosis
   of caterpillar
      to pig
to long-nosed armadillo;

having your heart squeezed
till it can bear no more,
then it's squeezed again;

breathless sunset
and dawn;

melody of silence;

rush
of the unspoken
   word.

Portrait of Dora Marr

In this portrait
Dora is woven
with the unnerving hues
of screeching clowns
and carnival candy.
But her raw-sienna lips
are locked in a viselike grip,
and a jagged
thunderbolt
crackles
across her blouse,
boding something
far more malefic
than simple
bad weather.

With a violet brushstroke
of manganese violet,
Picasso renders her
with the snout
of a *taureau*.
Crimson walls frame her,
like a coffin
lined in velvet,
but her eyes revolve

like a carousel
in a garishly lit
yet abandoned
amusement park.

Suddenly
she's alive,
and a limpid pool
of chromium-oxide green
darkens her face
as she glares
back
    at you.

Nothing but

Listen carefully.
Somewhere inside
you is a bull
with an elegant
molten snout.
And if you dare
    stare
into its bottomless gaze,
you will be trampled
by the force
of its overwhelming
    sagacity.

When you fall asleep,
completely unaware
of such creatures,
you'll encounter
a hoot owl
who defecates stones
etched with hieroglyphs
that not even the wisest
    of ants
can decipher.

When you awaken,

an insistent drone
of domesticated logic
will scream from
civilized heights
that owl stones
are simply made
from the crushed bones
   of birds
that they've devoured,
and that bulls
are filled with nothing
   but bullshit.

But the laughing black bear
and snickering coyote
know better.

Homeland

I am content
to stand before
the fathomless runes
of your eyes
until I go forth
like a jaguar:
stealthy in love
and sinister
in pursuit of prey.
I carry a god
in my belly,
and even in death
I cannot
    be overcome.

I travel like a bold,
    bright star:
circling the earth
as I carry you
on my shiny back
till we reach
the distant threshold
of our homeland.

Scène de tauromachie

A bull appears
to be grunting:
head upturned,
horns shaped
like inverted
question marks,
while a matador
lies frozen beneath
the burnt-umber hulk
of this elegant creature,
his hand still clutching
a gilded dagger
that never found
its quarry.

They lie there
like a pair of lovers
who have perished
in a moment
    of ecstasy.

Dressed like a coquette,
the matador's embroidered
tights and golden vest
glitter

under midday sun.
While the bull is adorned
with the ancient raiment
of blood
and is consumed
by an everlasting fire
   smoldering
in its coal-black eyes.

Nothing moves,
yet the earth resounds
with a steady pounding
   of hooves,
as matadors fly
like puppets tossed

through hot
dry
   air.

A promenade with Walt Whitman

When you walk with Walt
it's always daylight
and a bugle sounds merrily
    in the air.
His gait is slow,
deliberate,
    ponderous,
as if fearful of missing
some essential revelation
in the ebb and flow
of salt water,
or in the lilac
and her sudden bloom.

When you walk with Walt
it's always midnight,
as the stars scream
in a chill breeze
and a brook warbles
in the broken land
of Paumanok
    and Narragansett,
drowning the cry
of bayonets
that soak the field

with young men's blood,
and muffling even
the somber widows
and their savage lament.

When you walk with Walt
it's always sunrise,
and his gaze is like a child's:
overwhelmed by a myriad
of simple wonders,
marveling at dewy vapors
that rise above tombstones
on a dusty plain
or at the broad,
muscular reach
of a conductor
and his flawless engine
of roaring steel
    and steam.

When you walk with Walt
it's always sunset,
as a ferryboat gleams
under wavering torchlight
and feasting brigades
moisten their lips
with flagons

of cool dry wine,
and flags snap
over the slopes
   of Brooklyn,
while brown-faced sailors
ride a flood tide
past the ice floes
and racing riverside
on their swift
and endless journey.

The black turtle

What about
the black turtle,
who shines
with primeval light?
She regards everything
with a hook-nosed
disdain,
and at the slightest
provocation
   withdraws
into a hardened
   ebony cell,
content to allow
her fragile eggs
to bask unprotected
in glaring sunlight.
If only I had known her
during certain key moments
of my turtleless life!
I might have emulated
her slow, sage gait;
her unhesitating
disappearance
from other more
obnoxious beasts.

Even when paddling
underwater in pursuit
of liquid prey,
or in her awkward
lumbering
across high grass
and hot asphalt,
she remains impervious
to impatience,
gleaming with slime
    and with grace.

Three musicians

At a plain wooden table
   engulfed
in somber shadow,
three musicians,
separate and distinct,
are linked
   in a chorus
      of ecstasy.

They wear harlequin
triangles of red
   and gold,
or are hooded
   and robed
like ancient priests,
or are draped
in simple sheets
of dove white
   and cobalt blue.

In their hands
float implements
of magic:
flutes shaped
like daggers,

severed heads,
fractured violins.

Their faces
    are veiled
or hidden behind
terrible masks
that grimly summon
all created things
that have passed away.

They are messengers
    of death
in a shimmering world
of vanity.
They stare at us
from a place
of immortality
as their eyes beam
like a full moon
    freed

        from clouds.

Do you remember?

Do you remember
when even the stones
   spoke
and you returned
their greeting
without shame?
Drenched in sweat
under a sweltering
   August sun,
surrounded by petals
purple and white,
before the beasts
had abandoned you,
you traced the silver
jubilation
   of stars
and laughed
at the ridiculous clarity
of cratered moonlight.
Can you summon
   once more
the violent quarrels
of grasshoppers
who knelt before
your outstretched hand

as if paying homage
to a perfect turquoise god?
Can you still invoke
the bellowing
of turgid fireflies
dressed like luminous brides
about to be cast
into ecstatic convulsions?
Or will you regain
your proper powers and,
like a venerable father
attaining the summit
of a starry-eyed hill,
cast your gaze
as unencumbered
as a child
who turns his head
to behold
something new?

Queen Venus

Queen Venus!
With her moist
shiny hair
plastered over dewy lips,
and her bounding girlish
breasts leaking honey
and sweet ambrosia!
O,
slutty artful muse
of drunken sailors
and lost, broken boys
who stroke their
beating hearts
and dream
their vapid dreams
of plunder!
O,
Queen Tart!
Bent head-first
over my brass-balled bed,
stretched between
a bright loincloth of heaven
and a fresh
budding scent
of hell.

My arrow
is a warbling bird
that lands
with resounding
splash
as it cleaves
your watery nest!
You were always a virgin,
no matter how many
fiery storms
showered down
their boiling spray,
you who made dawn blush,
and sun and moon
rise and fall
with sinking heart,
aghast
at how you soothe
that mighty angel blast
O Venus,
my comely
love-strewn
Queen!

Night flowers

Armed with love
or with a cold hard
reach of steel,
we yearn
for a deliverance
that tantalizes
and eludes us
as we roam
with dimmed lamps
over a blighted earth,
enduring a torture
of lofty hopes,
while all around
young buds
bloom and droop
in shades of primrose
    and violet:
graceful tremulous creatures
bent with sorrow's
heavy load,
and swollen
with fierce golden
    roots:

Faint night flowers,

whose gentle persistence
in a scattered dawn
   mocks
the insurmountable strength
of brazen gods
immortal in their gait,
yet by simple men
soon to be
forgotten.

Cobra

A falcon-headed god
leads me by the wrist;
a jackal-headed deity
nibbles at my feet.
I walk on warm sand
in the shadow of a temple,
while chaste young virgins
with necklaces of turquoise
rub oil
on golden skin
and bask beneath
the luminous eye
of the sun.
As I observe
their artful gestures,
a black cobra
    slithers along
the back of my head,
its ruby tongue
    flickering
as it whispers:
"Every man
has three eyes;
and a jeweled crown
shines forth

with rays of pure light
that banish all darkness."

Turning round
I behold a gargantuan viper
   and flinch,
then apologize profusely:
"It was your awesome beauty
that struck me with fear."

"No," she corrects me,
"you were struck because
my gaze penetrated
your grotesque
and grinning mask,
beaming directly
into the wellspring
of your heart."

   She drops
and quivers
across the sand,
her crystal eyes merging
with the earth,
leaving only
a bundle of bones
wrapped in lace

and decorated
with pearly white
seashells.

The Foolish Joy of the Young Bull

Infinite proposition

The boys whiz by
on skateboards
    made of steel.
A sprightly young woman
in elegant heels
    clip-clops
through sunlight,
her skirt rippling lazily,
her legs firm stalks
of flesh marching
with regal gait.
The queen has replicated
herself endlessly,
and her minions,
as dumb as drones
insipidly droning,
fly in widening circles
with a disposition
of infinite ease,
like an ankh
           looping
     lethargically
back upon itself.

As the boys hover

in midair,
neither queen nor drone
is aware
of a single drop of nectar
that teases parched lips,
dangling

over a precipice.

Childhood on Brooklyn streets

Possessed by mischievous gods,
we played our sacred games
on Saturday afternoon asphalt,
a life-or-death
Roman arena intensity
burning
in our fiery eyes.
Schoolgirls in pleated skirts
hopscotched,
    hula-hooped,
       jumped rope,
or ring-around-the-rosy'd
as we whirled ecstatic
under blazing midday sun.
We celebrated
the festival of spring
by cutting bristles off
of old brooms with rusty saws,
wrapping the splintered ends
with electrical tape,
and slamming rubber balls
into a heaven
of tar-papered rooftop
or down to hell,
the sewers stinkier

than the foulest Styx.
This was fun,
this was fab,
this was all we knew.
Graced with wing'd
    roller skates,
we defied fin-tailed cars
doing eighty
on residential streets,
and somehow
no one was killed.
But on Independence Day,
Asclepius did a brisk business
mending exploded palms
and shattered fingertips,
the streets imbued
with sulfuric fireworks
and bedecked with tattered
cellophane wrappers
made in China.

Blood, gunpowder,
and whistling explosives:
What more
could a red-blooded
American boy
    ask for?

Sainte-Chapelle

Inside the jewel-box
cathedral
sunlight flickers
through golden dust.
Young boys gripping
their mothers
by the wrist
seem dazzled
as you walk by,
a ray of sunlight
captured in your eye,
the forest-green
of your soul
    unfathomable.

A *gardien*
blows a whistle;
the crowd parts
as you stroll past
medieval columns
of dove-gray limestone,
a few flakes
of celestial blue,
a few faint
five-pointed stars

still visible.

As we enter
the chapel of the dead,
I imagine your eye
     a crypt,
moss draped,
where I find
my eternal rest.

Perhaps this means
I knew all along
that you were killing me.

Thomas knew best what he knew least of all

Thomas always
had to be right.
No two ways about it:
he always (thought he)
     knew best.
He was a doubting Thomas
as regards anything
that slipped past
the slippery five senses.
Metaphysics and philosophy
were merely imaginary fish
swimming in maddening pools
     of insane brains;
Thomas had no doubt
about this or about being
a doubter.
He would argue not
with conviction
but with zeal:
not the same thing.
Zeal
is a fundamentalist illness,
a plague infecting
every level of society:
today's believers,

tomorrow's doubters,
yesterday's fishy madmen
all fundamentally
   the same.

At least Thomas
recognized the wonders
   of the world:
it's little natural miracles.
Deer,
snowflakes,
a child's awe,
a trilling bird.
But it's wonder
only seemed more awful,
more terrible,
when death struck
and suffering flesh
   cried out
in pain.

This poem is for Thomas.
There are no good answers;
just don't take God's
misdemeanors
personally,
Man.

E. E. Cummings' grasshopper

Tiptoeing into sunlight,
a grasshopper
glows
with a greenness
of unripe corn
and lands upon
      my book.

Flipping it
through the air,
I guide it gently
back to safety.

It crawls across the lawn,

      unburdened

            by alphabets.

Without her

Without her
a certain strength
    is gone,
that daily expectation
of love
vanquished:
not just eclipsed,
but erased.

They say
it was out of this void
that Vishnu
created the world
spawning a companion
who would one day
bring pain
and misery but also
a few fleeting

glimmers

of joy.

Haiku for Issa

Water lapping
  shoreline:
"Gulp! Gulp!"

Shouts the wind:
"You make too much
  of a splash!"

Poem for (our) fall

Rustle
   of restless
autumn leaves ~

      ~

        ~

I wish you were here
to see colors crisp
   and pure.
They tunnel out of earth,
transit every shade
of middle gray.
In nature there's no
"black or white,"
no absolute affirmation
or denial;
but instead
these middle tones:
an overlapping palette
of creation and destruction.

It cares not a whit
for you or I,
except to mirror
our every truth
   and lie.

Chambre

You were as unpredictable
as inclement weather;
as flashy as sunrise;
more *lunatique*
than a Full Beaver Moon.
Swirling tides waxed
      and waned
round the pools
of your tears.
Yet nothing could prevent
my attempt
to leap a wall
at your cottage garden,
climb your budding trellis,
and enter your tiny *chambre*,
where crumbs of ecstasy
were swept away
by a tumultuous
              rain.

Cosmogony

In the midst
of creating a world,
the gods take a cigarette break.
One blows smoke rings;
in turn, doughnuts,
wedding bands,
    and sinkholes
come into being.
A puff of smoke
    shaped
like a thundercloud
claps its hands
and rain falls,
causing even deities
to seek shelter
from the deluge.

During the storm,
to pass the time,
they invent parchment,
paste
and pixies,
who sharpen quill pens
with tiny teeth,
thus giving birth

to poetry.
Finally,
a fluted puff
grows into this form

Ψ

and parasols
come floating down.
"O, not for long,"
cried one divinity,
"will we smoke alone!"
Soon they were besieged
by an army of women,
who claimed the parasols
and, hand in hand,
led the gods away:
"There are worlds
    upon worlds,"
cried the women,
"and there's *work*
    to be done!"

"If only,"
moaned one immortal,
"amidst such smoke
    and mirrors,

we'd had the gift
   of foresight!"

"Even so," cried another,
"once she undid her dress,
would you ever
have imagined
what lurked beneath?"

And shaking their heads,
the gods went off
to pray.

Painting haikus

Blank canvas crouches
before looming brush,
fashioned from wild hog.

Unblemished canvas
awaiting a potent palette:
paintbrush moist, ready.

Luminous canvas
aglow with expectation:
demure, blushing.

Dew-dappled canvas
supine beneath rosy dawn,
fingered by sunrise.

Haiku for Basho

Proud cherry blossom,
star of haiku universe,
forever evanescent!

The foolish joy of the young bull

There's snow outside,
mocking the memory
   of sunshine.
Do seasons compete,
taunting and teasing
   one another,
or do they dream
of dovetailing with smooth
unassuming grace?
When snow melts,
does it more resemble
a trickle of teardrops
or a bursting riverrun
   of joy?

She had her seasons, too;
where merry spring
and burning summer
had, just moments before,
engendered new life,
now, only ice floes
and barren plains.
During a winter
of our discontent,
she bid a witch

to stick pins
into my waxen heart.
The miracle of ice
is that it ever dissolves.
But something happens
in the meantime,
between ourselves,
and since there's truth
   in wine,
among the drunken cups
of our hearts,
between the dog and wolf,
between the slaughter
of a sacrificial victim
and it being laid to rest,
eo ipso,
by that very act,
for her
it is an auspicious year.
(Woe to the conquered!)
For the pig teaches
the goddess of wisdom:
"I do not love you,
   and cannot
     say why."

Ibis

She lived
in the land
of the ibis
but was not
of sound mind.
She considered it
an ever-verdant paradise,
but I saw too clearly
the doorposts of innocents
       sprinkled
  with blood.
She dreamed I might become
an ibis-headed husband;
a fitting role, perhaps,
since I was not unschooled
  in disaster
and had learned quite early
how to console the wretched.
"Better as a bird surmounted
by a silvery moon,"
she reasoned,
"than the incarnation
of a mere ape or cat."

Fitting, perhaps, for Toth:

Egyptian god of knowledge,
science, and sorcery.
But in her presence,
shorn of my magic,
I felt more like
a flying kangaroo,
a hog in armor,
or a bull captured
with a decoy cow.
Sancta simplicitas!
There was nothing sacred
remaining except
a holy astonishment
over my own naiveté,
my guileless portrait
now rendered
in silver and gilt wood
and carved into a totemic
variety of bewildering
zoomorphic forms.

Please, speak to me
no more of *amour fou*,
that intoxicating poison
that has always
led me
      astray.

Tree

A tree
     shorn
  of its leaves

offers the sleek beauty

of bark

       in cold
          sunlight.

From the egg

Suddenly you're sixty,
and you gaze back
at the horror
and wonder
with an attitude
of humbled detachment,
shuttling between
fleeting rapture
and lingering bemusement.
"All things change,"
sagely says Heraclitus,
but the key is that
unchangeable thing
    inside
at the bottom
of the well:
A Well Being
we call
well-being.
Speak to it
and you'll know precisely
    what I mean.
From the beginning.
from the cradle,
from the origin,

from the egg,
let ill feeling be absent
from head to heel.
Even when abyss
calls to abyss,
one must anticipate
the morrow with eagerness
and give thanks
for those gifts
that make one precious.
Even when dangling
        at the point
    of absurdity,
let there be no ill omen.
For, as the love poet
Propertius has it,
"In great affairs,
it is enough
to have the will."

Yes, give thanks.

But never
cease to rage
against the gods.

The umbrellas of Cherbourg

The umbrellas of Cherbourg
   as seen from above
       twirl
like pastel-colored saucers
   hovering over
slick wet cobblestone.
Their shimmering hues
   dance
     in defiance
   of despair.

But Guy Foucher
paces beneath
a black umbrella.
In his hands he grips defeat.
His anguish sends him whirling,
yet only in abandonment
will he cobble together
   his heart.

Geneviève is garlanded
   with beauty;
no wonder a diamond merchant
hopes to set her like a stone
upon a ring.

As Roland whisks her away
    from Guy,
she falls into the trap.
For she remains unaware
that the sun is a blazing
    scarab beetle,
pushing a ball of dung
above a dusty ground.
This means:
only among common objects
may we find our proper place,
and even our joy,
despite the lofty measure
of the solar deity.
"It's strange
how sun and death
travel together," she says,
yet this brief insight
has arrived too late.

Geneviève once considered herself
"A girl who laughs at anything
and who says that love's a lovely thing."
But when Guy is rescued
    by Madeleine,
she's no longer smiling.

"We have chosen a life together,"
Guy explains while glancing
with admiration
at his new companion:
a woman who's never laughed
    about love
or grown enraptured
over lofty things.

Sometimes love
is not a given
but, instead,
is simply chosen.

The wine of youth

Once upon a time
we would while away
   the hours,
puffing on cigars
like nineteenth-century *flâneurs,*
strolling through life
as if it were an endless
   promenade.
Where we were going
or how we were getting there
was not our concern.
But beware!
By mid-journey
a gale may overtake you
despite your pharaonic collar
of quartz,
lapis lazuli,
green feldspar,
despite that lotus blossom
of colored glass
or your falcon's head
   of gold.
Yet, one must never forget:
Even when shedding
the countenance of youth,

as long as your lips are fleshy,
you'll don a turquoise crown
and grasp firmly
the poppy buds
of the queen
as she extends her hand
in the form of
   an ankh.

In ancient Egypt,
the hieroglyph for *life*
assumed the shape
of a *handheld mirror*:
where one gazes
to behold a fleeting miracle.

Osiris,
god of the dead,
has no business there.

What the Salamander Unleashed

Wobbling to and fro

Between iceberg and ship, effigies of wooden saints bob and weave ~ heaving in storm, cresting in foam ~ as darkness gives way to dawn.

"For beauty, I would drown."

"No, foolish boy. For love you would endure all, if only guaranteed another breath."

While tumbling waves plash rotting saints, all things weep and laugh, whether virginal shy or clenched in doom.

In distant lands a farm girl, lingering in shadow, is accompanied by a sad-eyed lap dog and a bellowing ass. Her mill, never idle, wobbles to and fro. She remains unaware of these saints driven by a swelling tide, grinding and pressing lips together. But she's proud of her mill, which processes neither wheat nor flour.

She rides the mill-wheel round and round and up down. Even in noontime brightness she grinds away, following the ebb and crest of foaming waves.

For, all things partake in a great love chain of being.

Gardener

It's not always easy to uncover a link between past and present.

At first she bore only a faint resemblance to the girl I once knew. Little did I realize that her mother had abandoned her after the fowls in the village had mysteriously perished.

Upon coming of age, she escaped to Paris. Strolling beside the Seine, she resembled a wide-eyed Madonna – stealing my attention from the looming cathedral and its clusters of ivy, cascading over high walls and churning in muddy water. Her gaze, veiled in tattered silk, wove its subtle deceit. For I was still a virgin to crude fetishes, morbid emotions, and ceremonies involving crocodile skin.

Eventually I lost all trace of her scent. Rumor had it that she'd vanished somewhere east of Transylvania.

When our paths crossed once again, she failed to inform me that her bed, covered in oak leaves, was infested with frogs. It wasn't until I visited her homeland that I learned the following:

While still in her early twenties, three times, sundials
cut from granite pointed to a rendezvous with
suicide. But she failed even in those tasks. Waking in
a hospital under blinding light, instead of being
grateful she felt exposed, though the doctors didn't
know the half of it. Pagans believe that stars are living
creatures, but the lamps in her orbs now effused a
gaslight glow.

Soon, a new plan was hatched. If she could convince
others to question their own sanity, then they'd be
forced to inhabit her weedy garden.

Creepers not uprooted in youth may result in
permanent infestation. Trunks thicken, runners swell,
tendrils sprawl. But when she enslaved me as her
gardener, she failed to inform me that my job was to
nourish weeds instead of destroying them. No
wonder the tools in her shed were rusted, antiquated,
broken.

After I drowned her creepers in a deluge of sulfur,
she let go her grip and bid me farewell. How was I to
know that she'd fallen in love with her own disease?
Once I escaped, thorny tendrils sprouted,
camouflaging the corpse of a misbegotten youth.

Only when I fired a musket at her feathered effigy did I become a man again: free.

Frozen in time

Yes: stare long and hard at the mirror of existence. But be careful what you focus on.

Perhaps Blake said it best: "I can stare at a knot in a piece of wood until I'm frightened of it" – and he wasn't kidding.

Once, peeking into an outhouse, I saw the Savior kneeling, sucking a prostitute's toe. Fatigued from walking disconsolate streets, she'd lost all hope; and he sought to reassure her, to assuage her pain.

Once, I stared at a rabbit till it froze. Before I could tender it a blessing, a fox crept up and walked off with his dinner – dangling from crimson fangs.

Once, when the men of the village were away carving wooden bowls, I crouched beside a girl hulling corn and pounding meal. Noting my presence, she gazed up and asked: "Are we going to be saved, or not?"

If you stare long and hard, a moment arrives when you realize:

We are the ones who will be eaten.

Architecture of melancholy

Entering a Parisian cathedral, I sat beside a pew of shriveled widows, draped in black. At first I hardly noticed them. I wasn't there to pray – heaven forbid! – but to admire architecture.

What was it that drew my attention from the vaulted Gothic arches to the widows' aching lament? Without warning, their melancholy welled up from floor to spire, filling the air with palpable heartbreak.

Over the years, those wizened women stayed with me, lingering in my breast like shadows flitting across dusty chapels. Harboring a stubborn hope – kneeling before a specter that dangled the prospect of deliverance if only they could utter a proper incantation – they put Pandora's box to shame.

Greek myth has nothing on them.

Hidden portrait

Perhaps you can imagine the artist, brush in hand, painting red and blue trees. But can you picture Paul Cézanne leaning headfirst into a winter wind, howling along Broadway and 42nd Street?

How would he digest those mountains of light: digital billboards, flashing at Times Square? No doubt, they would fascinate and confuse him. Such gargantuan displays! But lacking the luminosity of his tiny canvases. How explain it?

Once, disgusted by an all-consuming effort he'd expended upon perfecting a portrait, he tossed it into the branches of a nearby tree. He left it there for days, despite the rain, the wind, the beauty of his still-moist brushstrokes.

For one often dreams of abandoning the very thing to which we will sacrifice all.

Princess, snake

Don't be too impressed by the snake. He's here
simply to remind you of what crawls beneath the
surface.

Black is his royal color.
Purple, his majestic tongue.
Green, his eyes – the old rebirth routine.

His toxin heals the malcontent, but it's available only
to those willing to get down on hands and knees. If
you insist upon walking with your head in the clouds,
a bite will bring you to heel.

Since like attracts like, a princess who falls in love
with a serpent is imbued with cold blood and
possessed by a haughty demeanor – until she's
compelled to sleep with this slimy reptile.

But only if she sips its poison will she obtain the
treasured status of being a lowly human once again.

Leaping dogs of the dead

In a sunny cemetery she fed me grapes. Between weathered tombstones I imbibed her wine. Wild dogs howled as she peeled an orange, slice by gleaming slice, our lips wet and sticky.

Her laughter echoed on granite markers – those pointless souvenirs. Yes, she shamed the dead: the dead of Brooklyn, the dead that only know Brooklyn, and the "only the dead know Brooklyn."

Under setting sun we fell asleep, her hair the color of wheat. When we awoke, we were locked in the graveyard, but watched over by those faithful beasts. How many canines had leapt over our supine flesh?

Unlike Persephone, I had no desire to escape from the Underworld.

Why scarab beetles dance on balls of dung

On that day, Rome showed no mercy:

Smoldering fire, trails of ash, all hope extinguished. Tongues of gods severed at the root, slaughtered like pigs on a platter.

Wolves come up smelling like roses when compared to men.

Limpid-eyed girls seated at somber tables in a library, studying history's lengthening shadow. Money, murder, madness .... They turn the pages and yawn as squirrels scamper past sorcerers, and dragonflies hover over lakes of blood.

In a country of lost and broken roads, fables will one day be cataloged correctly, in the nonfiction section. And history books will find a proper place, between poetry and prose.

"Just keep your eye on that ball of dung, pushed by a patient beetle."

Portraits commissioned from afar

The dead may disappear without a trace, yet some continue to play hide-and-seek. Refusing to vanish, they take refuge in our dreams.

When I encounter them, they're often engaged in mundane affairs. An uncle dressed in a blue blazer from the 1930s returns to walk his beloved dog. A recently deceased companion is seated at a bistro table, eating spaghetti. But he's afraid to stand up – death has rendered him wobbly-legged.

It's as if they're on holiday from Hades, reenacting roles prepared for them for centuries.

Sisyphus was allowed to return to earth to arrange his own funeral. But the spirits of my acquaintance are often engaged in banal activities, as if posing for snapshots from everyday life. As the dreamer, I grow troubled, for these loved ones now appear incarnate – as if death never struck – yet I know this cannot be.

Eventually they disappear again. Decades pass until they pay another visit, but by then I harbor no doubt that they're truly disembodied. For they speak of unintelligible things and express no interest in returning to their mortal coil.

No mystery in that.

Wings

You shout at your own reflection in the mirror:

"So, you're in love again – idiot! You know how this
will end, don't you? Blazing along like a shooting
star, you imagine even the heavens are jealous of your
glory! You gaze longingly as your spine tingles,
without noticing that your waxen wings have begun
to melt. 'How could it be otherwise?' you effuse
ecstatic, gripping a gilded trophy with the eagerness
of a child fondling a toy.

"But when darkness descends, you plunge headfirst
into a miasma. It was all meant to be, all right. Now,
you're in your proper place – flat on your bottom!
Even worms are better off. At least they have a
purpose, tunneling through mire. But what good is a
man? He's merely victim of one illusion after another.
But after all, *someone* has to don those ersatz wings!

"Yes, you're in *love* ..."

Where were you leading me?

Mermaid, please. Don't judge me too harshly. I faithfully followed you into darkening depths, but it was difficult to keep up with the faint glow of your tail, undulating like a giant hand, waving goodbye.

Before you disappeared into a murky abyss, a single ray of light cut across my path in a pencil-thin line. It was my last chance. I could turn round and follow it up, to the ocean's lid, or else be forever lost in that pitch-black netherworld.

Besides, even you will admit:

There's a hint of danger in the way that you wiggle your hips.

A blink of time

The first man to ever love a woman – imagine his plight! For a moment the world seemed different. Objects assumed a strange glow; and, if he tugged at a thread, unexpected patterns appeared in its unraveling.

Imagine his grief when suddenly all this was lost. He could barely manage to cover her corpse with a blanket of wild grass. Even then – when men spoke only of fire, air, earth, water – somehow he realized that flowers must be gathered. That something in their blooming and wilting offered a fragrant yet bereaved correspondence.

All this occurred in a blink of time.

Jaded angels

In angels' ears the laughter of men echoes like shrieks of horror.

Theirs is an inverted world. They comprehend things we do not, for they view them properly, reversed in a mirror reflecting our sorry abode.

When cherubs hover beside infants, they perceive fully grown adults, crayons in hand, constructing blueprints replete with spherical eggs. Some fledglings die at noon, others at midnight. Some chase their own tails and drop from dizzying exhaustion. Others hatch into hardy young Turks with swollen cheeks.

They will confuse even the most jaded of angels.

Sophia

Upon awakening, Apollo would ask Sophia to gaze
out a window:

"What do you see?"

"Nothing."

But one day, while composing alchemical texts,
Hermes took a long swig of whiskey. His eyes
blurred: he mistook salt for sulfur as mercury slipped
between his fingers and the Divine Fire broke through
a glass beaker. And then a goat was heard to cry out.

"What is it?" Apollo growled, awoken from his
slumber.

"A goat," Sophia replied, "braying with birth pains."

"That boy Hermes must finally have begun his
work."

From this bellowing beast, everything came out from
hiding. It gave birth to wands, swords, cups,
diamonds.

"A real mess," sighed Sophia. "What are you going to do?"

"I'm going to visit my mother."

"Typical Greek!"

The following morning, Sophia was abandoned to a wilderness terrorized by a monstrous jackal. But she was said to be clever. She fenced herself in around four stockade posts garlanded with morning glory.

When the jackal arrived, it poked and prodded, testing every crevice and humping every hole, but it couldn't break through.

"My enclosure is shut tight – impenetrable – in spite of your enormous length and girth." Sophia taunted. "Nowhere is there another woman like me. Abandoned by the gods, yet I refuse to make a pact with evil!"

But the hungry jackal was not to be outwitted. The next evening it snuck back and ate the morning glory, then disguised its voice to resemble that of a young girl. Sophia was convinced that she'd found a heartfelt companion: "Just like me, she's a darling jettisoned into the wild!" But when she undid the stockade, she was eaten alive.

Meanwhile, Apollo had consulted with his mother to ask for Sophia's hand in Divine Marriage. But now, all he found were her bones, strewn carelessly about. With ax and spade, he buried her defiled remains. To this day, women bereft of God come knocking on her grave:

"Come out; come out!" they chant.

"Go away; go away!" Sophia intones from beneath the earth. "Not even jackals would care to dance with my bloody skeleton. There's nothing left!" But the women are insistent:

"We love you more than God!"

Glory sur la quai

A look of resignation burns across the face of the sun. Perhaps it's set one time too many. To a child, it's merely the raiment of a bright morning. But to you, the mourning of another day, gone forever.

You linger at the riverside to await passage on a vessel sailing downstream. Two dour merchants, one selling balloons, the other cotton candy, leer at you with envy.

Then a girl holds out a dandelion, limp in her tiny hand.